THE ROOT REMAINS

By

Tiffany Lindsey

Copyright

The Root Remains

By Tiffany Lindsey

ISBN: 978-0-578-79118-0

Cover design by Denise M. Walker (Armor of Hope Writing & Publishing Services, LLC)

Editor: Armor of Hope Writing & Publishing Services, LLC

Printed in the United States of America

Dedication

This book is dedicated to my children, your children and children all over the world.

Prologue

It's easy to see the result of something, but we often don't look into what happened to cause it in the first place. Whether you are a parent or you work with or interact with children, my prayer is that you choose to see beyond and choose to dig deeper to the *root*.

Table of Contents

Introduction

⊲◆⊳

Fruits and Trees

    A woman planted a seed, watered it, nurtured it, and soon it began to grow roots. The roots became the foundation of a pear tree that resulted from a pear seed. As the tree continued to grow, it eventually yielded pears. The woman saw this and grew sad and disappointed. She did not want pears. Instead, she wanted apples. After noticing the tree continued to produce pears, she set out to make the tree have apples. First, she took off all the pears. Then, she found apples and tape. She tried to tape the apples to the tree, but they fell off. She tried placing them in spaces where the apple could fit, but the apples would roll out of the tree and land on the ground. Eventually, she found a substance that would make the most difficult things stay put and it worked. Later on, she went back to the tree. The apples were still there but so were the pears. Frustrated, she walked away and gave up because she knew of nothing else she could do.

The Process of Growth

    Have you ever tried to plant anything? I don't really have a green thumb. The last time I remember planting anything was when I was in elementary school. We were learning about ecosystems and had made our own for both plants and animals. Let me just say that doing both, taking care of both was a lot!

    The growth process is by no means as simple as planting a seed and watching it grow. There is a process, and believe it or not, the life and death of that seed depends on it. Although there are seeds that can grow under harsh conditions, the majority need extra care. Soil is needed when planting a seed. After finding soil, you place the seed into it and it begins. The work is not complete but merely beginning, as you provide water, sun, and anything else the seed needs. Some seeds may take longer than others to grow, but if you continue the process of nurturing the seed, it will happen. If you don't take care of the seed by giving it what it needs, more than likely, it won't grow. If it does, the plant may not be as healthy or as strong as it could have been had it gotten the things that it needed to thrive.

Let's go back to me being in elementary school. My science teacher had to teach us how to take care of the animals and plants. We did not know how to on our own. If we tried to by ourselves, I am pretty sure nothing would have lived and if it did, it would not for very long. However, the more we were taught the more we learned. As a result, because of what we were taught, the plants we had thrived and the animals not only survived, but they thrived as well. As much as we try to on our own, we cannot do what we haven't been taught.

Children and Roots

We are sadly mistaken if we think that the same thing does not apply to children. Some of our children already have seeds in them before they even come into this world while others get different seeds planted inside of them throughout childhood. Ideally, you want to plant seeds that bring about good and positive things. You want to plant seeds of confidence so that they know who they are and embrace themselves. You want to plant seeds of belief so that they know anything is possible. For some children, those seeds are planted and nurtured but so are seeds of negativity. Seeds of negativity can be identified as any and everything that can have a negative impact on a child. Some examples are seeds of doubt, fear, low self-esteem, and more. As parents, educators, and adults who interact with children, we are all planting something, whether we know it or not.

When Seeds Turn to Fruit

Nurture a seed long enough, and it will grow, regardless of the type of seed it is. As that seed grows, it will eventually yield fruit. It is at this moment we see the behaviors, mannerisms, and actions that are a result of what was planted. A child wants to commit suicide and has even attempted it because they feel like they don't matter. Their low self-esteem, accompanied by bullying by their peers, only added fuel to a flame that was already burning. Another child has now transitioned into adolescence and has started to show promiscuous behavior. When she was a child, she was molested for years by someone she knew. When she finally told someone she trusted, they did not believe her. By keeping so much in and never healing from her previous experiences, she eventually began to act out, and she is now in her current situation.

So far, I hope I've been able to get you to understand what I mean when I say the *root*. On the next few pages, there are children from various age groups that go through different circumstances. Some may bring up different emotions for you. You may be able to resonate with one child. You may feel disappointed, angry and even sad. They are fictitious characters. As I mentioned before, their circumstances can and have happened in real life. Imagine if you were in their shoes. Maybe you have been. Even if you haven't, you may know someone who has.

Seen and Unseen

Sarah

Age Fourteen

"I am Sarah. I am five months pregnant, and I'm only fourteen. As I walked around the grocery store one day, a woman looked at me and made a remark to her friend. She noticed my belly, then looked at my face, seeing that I was obviously young. 'I'm so over seeing these babies having babies. Do they not know that having a child so young will ruin not only their life but their child's life as well? Too many mothers and not enough wives — it's ridiculous!'

"I heard her. I heard that woman, and she isn't the first to say something about my growing belly. My mother had me when she was thirteen. After that, she had a child, if not every year, at least every two years. By the time I was seven, I had to help. I had to help get my brothers and sisters dressed. I had to help make food. I felt alone. My mom was either out working or out with her friends. That's when I was left in charge, which was often. I didn't have many friends at all until I met him.

When we met, he was nice, and he listened to me. He was three years older than me, but he said that didn't matter to him. So, I figured it didn't need to matter to me either. I had no one who truly cared, but he did. After losing my virginity to him while my mom was out again, he invited me over and I went.

The next thing I know, I started feeling weird. I started to feel like I had to throw up, but I never did. Three months went by, and my period still did not start. I told him. I thought since he had always been there he would be there this time. The day I told him was the last time I've seen him or talked to him. I've tried calling him and even being in the places I thought he would be, but I never saw him. He'd told me places he usually would hang out at, but I guess that was a lie.

After not being able to see him or find him, eventually, I gave up and decided to come clean and tell my mom. The night I told her she just stared at me and said she had to go out, but before she left, she mouthed four words to me . . . 'Get rid of it.' That was a few weeks ago, and things are still the same.

The next time my mom talked about it she told me that we were going to get rid of it. I know what I did was wrong, but I couldn't, and I told her. She told me it was either me or my baby, and as hard as it was, and how much harder I knew it was going to be, I told her, again, I was going to keep my baby. She told me to get out. I couldn't take anything but the clothes off my back as I was pushed away from a place that I would no longer be able to call home. After hearing what she said, I shrugged it off like I didn't care but I did. Her words hurt me . . . I was hurting."

Statistics

According to the Center for Disease Control:

- In 2015, a total of 229,715 babies were born to women aged 15–19 years, for a birth rate of 22.3 per 1,000 women in this age group.

- Less favorable socioeconomic conditions, such as low education and low-income levels of a teen's family, may contribute to high teen birth rates.

- Teens in child welfare systems are at higher risk of teen pregnancy and birth than other groups.

  - https://www.cdc.gov/teenpregnancy/about/index.htm

Reflection

What would you have done as a child if you were in Sarah's shoes? How would you have felt?

_____

_____

_____

_____

_____

If you had the chance to meet Sarah, what would you tell her?

_____

_____

_____

_____

_____

Michael

Age Ten

"How old is Michael?"

"Oh, he's ten years old."

"He's ten, really? Aren't kids his age usually a lot more active?"

"Yeah, he's pretty quiet."

"Why, so you mean to tell me this kid doesn't talk to anyone?

"Oh no, he talks to Jermaine."

"Oh, really?"

"Yeah."

"Oh alright."

***

"I hate it when Mr. Jermaine isn't at the center. The other workers are nice, but they aren't him. Adults sometimes make it seem like they care, but soon you find out they really don't. I got tired. I got tired of my mom seeing me and seeing my dad. She once told me that I would grow up to be just like him. I don't have many memories of him, but my mom seems to have them for the both of us. She said my dad never cared about me or her and left when I was three years old. She asks me all the time do I remember, and I tell her no. Then, she goes on and on with her alcohol in one hand and a cigarette in the other. This happens every time she gets drunk — she goes on and on, then begins to yell.

"I remember one time she got so drunk. I had just got back from the community center, and she was crying, looking at an old album that I hadn't seen in years. I asked her what she was looking at, and she told me nothing but to get ready for dinner. As I started making my way to my room, she said, 'You look just like him. Same hair, same eyes, same nose, same skin, same ears — he's you, and you're him.'

"After that, things got really loud. She got up, almost tripped, and started walking toward me calling me my dad's name. She started shoving her finger at me, pointing out the same things she said we had the same. I started asking her if she was okay and tried to take the bottle out of her hand, as she was still falling, when she smacked me and told me to never touch her drink. All she had to do was tell me once, and I never did it again.

Mom didn't hit me again since then, but she still has her moments. When that alcohol and cigarettes get her going, it's hard for her to calm down. So, I learned to stay out of the way. Seems like from what my mom said, I was in my dad's way, and now, I'm in her way too. To stay out of her way, I just stay in my room. Even when I'm not where she is having her fit, she still yells at me. I can still hear her, so I put my headphones on and listen to music. Music for me is an escape at home, and it was when I went to the center.

Then, Mr. Jermaine started working there. Some of the teachers tried talking to me, but eventually, they stopped after I still didn't say anything to them. Mr. Jermaine tried to do the same thing, but he was different. He saw me with my headphones and asked me what I was listening to, after days of me not talking to him. I turned my music even louder, and I guess he could hear it because he started rapping to the same song I was listening to. That was the day Mr. Jermaine and I became friends."

Statistics

According to Childhelp.org:

- A report of Child Abuse is made every 10 seconds.

- Every year more than 3.6 million referrals are made to Child Protective Agencies.

- In 2014, state agencies identified an estimated 1,580 children who died as a result of abuse and neglect — between four and five children a day.

https://www.childhelp.org/child-abuse-statistics/

Reflection

What would you have done as a child if you were in Michael's shoes? How would you have felt?

_____

_____

_____

_____

_____

If you had the chance to meet Michael, what would you tell him?

_____

_____

_____

_____

_____

_____

Dawn

Age Thirteen

"Why Dawn always gotta dress like that? asked Tonya."

"I know, right, and she's always in some boys face," Michelle responded.

"She's what my momma calls a fast girl."

"What's a fast girl?"

"A fast girl is a girl just like Dawn."

"Oh okay, I don't ever want to be like that."

"Dawn," Mrs. Smith calls.

"Here," I reply. Then, I hear someone smack their lips, and I know exactly who it is. She doesn't like me because all the boys like me. I chuckle and turn around to glare at her for a little longer than a second and turn back around after she rolls her eyes. I have one friend, but everybody else here doesn't like me. But whatever, I can't help how I am or how I look. Today is like every other day: home, bus, school, bus, home. Me and my friend sit next to each other on the bus — she gets off before I do because her stop is closer. My stop is just a few more blocks down. The bus finally makes it to my stop, and I pick up my backpack, put it on my back, and head down the walkway to get off the bus.

"Dawn, yo' momma ain't home. She left wit' ole' dude." I look to see who's talking to me, and it's the neighbor from around the way. Did he really have to say that out loud so everybody could hear? I know a lot of people see what's going on, but they don't need to hear about it, too.

"As usual, my homework is finished before Mom finally makes it home with whoever she left with. I hear a door slam and peek my head out of my room to see that momma has made it home with her boyfriend. I later hear a knock on the door, and momma asks if I ate already and did my homework. I tell her I finished my homework but didn't eat yet. I ask her if she is going to make something tonight. Before I could finish talking, she says, 'We ate already.' I asked her if she brought something, but she says they didn't and that I would have to go in the kitchen and fix something for myself.

"I'll make myself something," I say.

"This is the third night in a row. Her and her boyfriend go out doing things and eating out, but I don't get nothing. Every time my mom gets a new boyfriend, this happens. When it's me and her, she's different, but when someone else comes along, it's like she changes. I wipe away my tears before making it to the kitchen. The last time I let my mom see me cry I learned.

I have learned that no matter how much you cry, no one cares. No matter how pretty you think you are, there is always someone prettier than you. You may be hurting, but never let them see you hurt. It's why I wipe my own tears. It's why I try so hard to make sure I'm better, to make sure I look better, dress better. I guess it's working because the girls at school don't like me, but the boys like me. I guess it's okay. I'll be okay."

Statistics

According to Mom Junction:

- One of the first and main environment, your child will experience is the one at home.

- Since her birth, the emotional environment she sees and feels around her will shape her personality. The bond your child shares with you will help her understand and learn how to express her love and fears.

- The environment at your home and the relationship with neighbors will also affect your child's behavior.

- If you live in an environment that is overcrowded or is too loud, it can negatively impact your child's personality.

http://www.momjunction.com/articles/environment-influence-on-child-growth_00332016/#gref

Reflection

What would you have done as a child if you were in Dawn's shoes? How would you have felt?

_____

_____

_____

_____

_____

If you had the chance to meet Dawn, what would you tell her?

_____

_____

_____

_____

_____

_____

Brandon

Age Fourteen

"I think what has happened to Brandon is unfortunate, but it's not the first time I'm seeing it. Plenty of times I've seen young boys coming in, and they're in here because they appeared to be one way to one person, but I see it differently.

Man, it's been a few months since I've been here, and I've been ready since the first night to get out. It's hard, but I'm in here. I'm in here with boys who have done much worse than me. Sooner or later, you find out why people are here. A couple of boys are in here for assault and some attempted murder, but I'm here for using drugs. Ain't nobody been here to see me since I been here. I never knew my dad, so it's always been me, my mom, and my little sister. At one point, my mom was working three jobs. She had one she worked during the day, one during the night, and one on the weekends. It was mostly just me and my sister, so I took care of her.

I remember the day my mom was fired from one of her jobs, and she didn't know what to do. Being the man of the house, I had to step up, once again, like I did before. It's not hard to find drugs when you're living in my neighborhood — on every corner, there's somebody selling. It's easy to get, and it's easier to sell. So, I did.

I was put on to a dealer through a classmate, and the rest I guess you could say is history. I went months without being caught, but mostly, I was helping out my mom. She knew, I think she knew, what I was doing to get the money, but she didn't complain — she just took the money. It was all good and everything until she started spending extra money and quit her jobs. She said that she had been struggling to take care of me, so now it was time for me to take care of her. So, I kept selling. I didn't do it for her anymore, though. I did it for my sister — she needed me. I think my mom loved us, and she tried, but she never really showed it.

After I started selling, I joined a gang. Territory is a big thing, and I've seen people killed over space that they didn't know they were supposed to be in. I didn't want to end up like them, so I got protection. I got a family. They said they would be there for me, that they would be down for me as long as I was down for them. I've been told many lies before by friends and even my own momma, but I felt I could trust them. They were down for me for a bit, but then, I guess now they're not. Since I've been in here, none of them came to see me. I didn't want to be a snitch, so I ain't say nothing. It's my first offense, so it won't be too long til I'm out of here. But what do I do when I get back home? I wonder how my little sister is doing. I hope she's taken care of."

Statistics

- Mental health needs are often urgent for adolescents in the justice system. Many have mental illness (estimates range as high as 70 percent, with prevalence among girls as high as 80 percent, compared with 20 percent among the total adolescent population.

- Suicide rates in juvenile detention facilities are more than four times higher than for adolescents overall.

- According to a national survey conducted in 2012, an estimated 10 percent of young people in juvenile facilities reported sexual victimization by staff members or a peer.

https://www.childtrends.org/indicators/juvenile-detention/

Reflection

What would you have done as a child if you were in Brandon's shoes? How would you have felt?

_____

_____

_____

_____

_____

If you had the chance to meet Brandon, what would you tell him?

_____

_____

_____

_____

_____

_____

_____

Asia

—◁◆▷—

Age Seven

"**A**sia is a good student once you get past her behavior. I think her behavior is a cry for help. I've been teaching for the past fifteen years, and I have only seen this type of behavior with one other student. As a teacher, by law, when you suspect abuse, you are to report it. I don't think Asia is getting abused now, at least I hope not, but she has definitely experienced something. I try to talk to her when I can. I've met with her foster mom a few times, and she's told me all she knows about her. But she doesn't know everything. I don't think anyone knows everything there is to know about Asia. She isn't a student who is happy to open up much about anything. The bell rings and it's time to start class. There she is with an escort.

'Asia got into trouble for putting her hands on another student.'

'Okay, thank you for letting me know.' I look at her, and there she is, hands crossed in front of her, full of spunk and attitude. It looks like Asia and I will be having another talk. After giving out assignments, she's the first to finish, so I take my chance to see if she wants to talk. 'Come here, Asia. I want to talk to you.' She pulls up a chair to my desk and stares, then starts to pick at her nails. 'What happened'

'He was talking about me, so I hit him.'"

***

"What did we say about what to do when people talk about you?" my teacher says. I hear my teacher, and I can tell she cares. She listens to me, but I learned early in life to defend myself because no one else will. I've been in three different foster homes since I was two years old, and I'm only seven. I don't remember much of anything but the bad things. I was taken from my momma because she was on drugs. The kids at my old foster home found out and started calling me a *crack baby*. I told my foster mom what they were saying, and she laughed and told me they were right and that my momma didn't want me. I used to cry every time they were mean to me. I didn't stay there long, though. My foster mother told my caseworker I cried too much and said I was mentally challenged.

I got put into another foster home, and it seemed fun in the beginning. A lot of times my foster momma's nephew would come around and watch us when she had to do her stuff. He seemed really nice, too. We would all play games together. It was me and four other kids there, but I was the youngest. He was really nice to me until that day.

One day, I was sick, so I stayed at home with my foster mom. She got an emergency and didn't know who to call. Her nephew had stopped by to drop a few things off when she asked him to watch me until she got back. I didn't know he was there until she came and told me he was. Her nephew came into my room and sat on the bed and asked me how I was. I told him I wasn't feeling good, and he put his hand on my forehead to check if I had a fever. He said I was hot, then touched my arm, my chest, and my belly. He asked how I felt now, and I told him I still didn't feel good. I turned to my side, and he turned me back over and started doing things he was never supposed to do. That day I felt sick, but after what he did, no amount of medicine could make me feel better. I never told anyone.

'Asia, are you okay? Why are you crying?'

I look at my teacher, the only one who has listened to me and decide to tell her why I was angry, why I was crying. 'He touched me.'"

Statistics

- 1 in 5 girls and 1 in 20 boys is a victim of child sexual abuse.

- Self-report studies show that 20% of adult females and 5-10% of adult males recall a childhood sexual assault or sexual abuse incident.

- According to a 2003 National Institute of Justice report, 3 out of 4 adolescents who have been sexually assaulted were victimized by someone they knew well.

http://victimsofcrime.org/media/reporting-on-child-sexual-abuse/child-sexual-abuse-statistics

Reflection

What would you have done as a child if you were in Asia's shoes? How would you have felt?

_____

_____

_____

_____

_____

If you had the chance to meet Asia, what would you tell her?

_____

_____

_____

_____

_____

_____

Out of all the children and their stories, which one relates to you most and why?

_____

_____

_____

_____

_____

_____

_____

Time to Dig

If we want change to happen, if we want to see different fruits, then we must deal with the root. It isn't enough to yank off fruit and toss it away to be discarded. It isn't enough to try to cover it, and it isn't enough to pretend as though it isn't there. The fruit is going to continue to show until we begin to dig and uproot what has become the result of the seed. We see the what, but we forget to ask why -- we forget to look deeper beyond what we can't see. It is then, and only then, when we face it, that we will not just see a temporary change but a change that lasts. The next time you hear a story on the news, or the next time you hear a story about a child who may be having challenges, what will you think? Will you say something negative or think negative thoughts, or will you stop just a little bit longer to show some compassion and wonder if maybe, just maybe, there is more to what is happening than what it seems?

Epilogue

I hope that what was shared will help you or someone you may know. The person you help could either be an adult or a child. It is so important that we are all aware of the seeds that have been planted in us and the seeds that we plant in others, especially children.

About the Author

T iffany Lindsey is a wife and a mother from Houston, Texas. Tiffany loves working with children and has done so for the past decade.

As an educator and an ABA therapist, with children from different backgrounds, she has gained a variety of experience and knowledge. Tiffany believes that all children matter and that what we say and do as adults make an impact on their lives.

www.ingramcontent.com/pod-product-compliance
Lightning Source LLC
Chambersburg PA
CBHW061759040426
42447CB00011B/2383